Poor Richard

by Stef Schumacher

illustrated by Dick Smolinski

Chapters

Orlando Boston Dallas Chicago San Diego

Visit *The Learning Site!*

www.harcourtschool.com

Meet Ben Franklin

Ben Franklin was an important figure in American history. He helped to form the government of the thirteen colonies. He helped to write the Declaration of Independence. He also signed it. The Declaration of Independence said that the thirteen colonies in America should be free from British rule. This started the colonies down the road to freedom.

Franklin also contributed to the U.S. Constitution. He was one of the signers of this important paper that marked the beginning of the United States.

Ben Franklin was also an inventor of many useful things. He invented the bifocal lens. Glasses with these lenses let people see up close and far away. He invented a wood stove that made more heat than other wood stoves but used less fuel. Franklin stoves are still used today.

He experimented to prove that lightning was a form of electricity. He invented the lightning rod, a metal rod put on a roof. If lightning strikes, it hits the rod instead of the building.

When Ben Franklin was young, he enjoyed going to school. Unlike today, though, school was very expensive. At only ten years old, Ben had to leave school and go to work. He helped his father make candles.

Even though Ben could no longer attend school, he kept learning. He read books. He worked on his writing. He asked many questions and learned from the world around him.

When Ben was seventeen, he left Boston and went to Philadelphia. In the early 1700s, Philadelphia was the largest city in the British colonies. It was an exciting place to live and work. Ben soon found a job with a printer.

In his early twenties, Franklin opened his own print shop. He created a newspaper called *The Pennsylvania Gazette*. It soon became very popular and had many faithful readers.

Ben Franklin's newspaper was a success. He then went on to an even greater success. In 1733, he published *Poor Richard's Almanack.* It had a lot of general information. It also contained many wise and clever sayings that illuminated important truths.

Ben Franklin was a curious man who knew a great deal. His knowledge helped him give good advice. People loved reading *Poor Richard's Almanack,* and it soon became a best-seller.

Poor Richard's Almanack

Poor Richard's Almanack was written long ago, yet many of its sayings are still true today. In the *Almanack*, Franklin summons his readers to think about their own lives as they read his sayings and advice.

You can read some of Franklin's sayings in the pages that follow. They are fun to think about and talk about. Ask yourself how each saying applies to life in the twenty-first century.

Early to bed and early to rise, makes a man healthy, wealthy, and wise.

This saying is about healthful living and how it helps you get ahead in life. Getting up early and going to bed early are good for a person. Getting enough sleep keeps you healthy. When you are feeling good, you can get a lot done. Getting up early gives you the whole day to work. You can use this time to make money and to learn new things.

Do you think this is good advice? Do you get enough sleep? Do you get up early enough to get a lot done?

Little strokes fell great oaks.

Chopping down a huge oak tree is hard work! It takes many little strokes of an ax to cut the tree down. This saying tells us that a big job can be done in little steps.

Think of a time when you had to do a big report or project. How did you break this big job up into smaller parts? What might have happened if you had tried to do it all at once?

Lost time is never found again.

This reminds us to use our time wisely. When we waste time, it is gone forever. Those lost seconds and minutes add up to hours—even days.

Have you ever played around instead of doing your homework? Did you then have to do your homework in a big hurry? Have you ever missed out on something because you wasted time? Did you wish you could get those hours back again?

When the well's dry, we know the worth of water.

Sometimes we don't know how fortunate we are to have something. We don't understand how important it is until after it's gone or changed. This saying reminds us not to take things for granted.

Today, many people understand that important natural resources, such as water and oil, are limited. They know that we need to use them with care. Have you ever noticed how valuable something was only after it was gone?

No gains without pains.

This saying lets us know that hard work is important. To do something well, we must work hard at it. Working persistently will be rewarded in some way. We might gain by being paid for a job well done. We might also gain joy from hard work.

Have you ever exercised and had sore muscles later? This saying might be good for athletes in training. What do you think?

Speak little; do much.

This saying tells us several things. Sometimes actions are more important than words. It's all right to talk about what you're going to do. Sometimes, though, it's better to take action. A quiet person's actions can set a good example.

Have you ever set an example for others? Have you ever worked without saying much about it?

A true friend is the best possession.

Possessions are things that we have or own. A true friend is one who is faithful, no matter what happens. Having a faithful friend is worth more than owning valuable things.

Do you think having a good friend is important? Is being a true friend to someone else important?

Haste makes waste.

Sometimes rushing through a job causes problems. When people rush, they often do a poor job. Mistakes may happen. Things may have to be redone. It is usually faster and better to do the job correctly the first time.

Have you ever rushed through homework? Have you ever hurried while doing an art project? Did you make mistakes and have to start all over again? How much time did you waste by hurrying?

From 1733 to 1758, Ben Franklin published a new edition of the *Almanack* yearly. Each year he added clever sayings. Many generations of Americans since that time have enjoyed reading his good advice.

Ben Franklin always worked hard for his community and for his country. He knew that "lost time is never found again." Throughout his life, he tried to make the very best use of every single second.